# The Pocketbook of Prompts

## 52 Ideas for a Story

The Fine Line Editorial Consultancy

65 Lorne Street

Edinburgh

EH6 8QG


Published by The Fine Line

ISBN: 978-0-9567610-0-2

For Texas, Carolina, Georgia, Minnie,
and dad.

# INTRODUCTION

The Pocketbook of Prompts began as a series of weekly writing prompts, sent to subscribers of The Journal, the Fine Line newsletter. Each week, writers emailed, telling me they'd found them enjoyable, heartening, fun, saddening, frustrating, and inspiring. Some said they'd recommended them to their students, and others asked if they could use them in lessons. One woman said contemplating the questions raised by a prompt on everlasting life had given her the basis of her next book. Stories and contemplations arrived in my inbox. Something, it seemed, had been stirred in the imaginations of these writers. In response, I have put together a year's worth of prompts to form this collection of 52 ideas for a story.

At the back you'll find blank pages to make notes or to write a vignette sparked by a prompt. The collection doubles as a notebook – an invaluable tool for every writer.

The purpose of the prompts is to encourage writers to explore, both within and without themselves. They are designed to encompass key aspects of the writing process: research, point of view, description, character, plot, and dialogue, for example. They encourage writers to take concepts with which they thought they were familiar and make of them something new – something fresh, unexpected, unique, and their own. They challenge writers to step outside of the familiar.

Whether you are a writer, a teacher, or simply interested in the process of writing, you can use the prompts in any way that you wish – whether as a starting point for a novel, for discipline, for practice, for an enjoyable way of building on talent and desire to write, or for a way in which to put off writing that still feels like you're doing something productive.

Writing is a skill, a craft, an art, and a profession. It's hard work, but it's also exciting work. It is an adventure and so your approach to it should be adventurous. Contemplate ideas that have never before occurred to you. Look at language for the remarkable tool that it is. Relearn it as something that provides you with the ability to create anything in this or any other world. Enjoy yourself and never stop looking for that spark, often found in the most surprising places. I hope you find some here.

Kate Gould

# THE PROMPTS

# ONE

In 2003 a skeleton was found on a waste land in Rome. Beside it were a bunch of keys and a charred wallet. Although the bones were laid out to resemble a single human body, they were found to originate from at least five different bodies. The mystery may never be solved. Write your own story behind the skeleton. Who were the five people? Who killed them and why? Why did he or she lay the bones out to resemble a single skeleton? Are there five more composite skeletons to be found? The keys and wallet belonged to a man who remains missing, but tests have shown none of the bones belong to him. What has happened to him?

# TWO

A climactic scene in a classical romance: a squire is declaring his love to a fair maiden. Write it as it would occur in a work of this literary tradition. Then rewrite it, parodying it by introducing elements that are out of place and not in keeping with the scenario in its conventional form. The reader may think they know what to expect from the scene because it is familiar from other work so think of ways to create surprise and make the scene your own. It isn't necessary to ridicule the genre – just find ways to make it surprising.

# THREE

Beginning on August the 25th, 1835, the New York Sun published a series of articles about the discovery of life on the moon. The discoveries were said to have been reprinted from The Edinburgh Journal of Science and attributed to the well-known astronomer, Sir John Herschel. The author of the articles was Dr Grant, Herschel's amanuensis, who wrote that, using an enormous and innovative telescope, Herschel found trees, flowers, beaches, lakes, quartz pyramids, herds of bison-like creatures with hairy veils like a cap over their eyes, springing goats, pelicans, spherical amphibians rolling across beaches, volcanoes, beavers that walked upright and lived in huts, elks, horned bears, miniature zebras, winged humanoids, sapphire temples, a number of civilized tribes, and works of art. The articles were later revealed to be a hoax. Herschel had made no such discoveries, Dr Grant was fictitious, and the real author of the articles was not revealed.

Create your own hoax. Write about an event or give an explanation for a phenomenon either real or imagined. See how plausible you can make it sound. The New York Sun's hoax may sound preposterous now, but it was widely believed at the time and Herschel received many enquiries from people asking for further details about his discoveries.

# FOUR

You're driving along a deserted road, miles from anywhere, when you see a wedding dress hanging from a tree. How did it get there?

# FIVE

A man has committed a murder and has just dumped the body in a lake. Without mentioning the murder, describe the lake from his point of view. Use the description to reveal his thoughts and feelings. You could write this in a number of ways. For example, write it in the first person. You could write it in the third person as though he were being observed by an omniscient narrator. You could broaden the scenario and try writing it from the point of view of someone else at the scene. The person watching might have been involved in the murder. He or she might not have been involved but saw the man dumping the body in the lake. Alternatively, he or she might not know anything about the murder or body and just happened to see the man while walking by the lake. Remember not to mention the murder.

# SIX

The fairytale, Hansel and Gretel, is usually told in the third person with the assumption that the children and their father are good while their mother and the old woman who seeks to fatten and eat Hansel are bad. Change the perspective and rewrite it in the first person from the perspective of the children's mother. What motives might she have had to send the children out into the forest? Did she know about the old woman? If so, how did they meet? Is she actually a baddie in the tale or just misunderstood? Rewrite the tale in any way you like - change the setting and denouement, for example - but make sure you write it entirely from the point of view of the mother.

# SEVEN

You get up one morning to find a Dear John letter on your kitchen table from someone you thought died 10 years ago. What does it say?

# EIGHT

Who lives in this house?

# NINE

This began as a Valentine's competition, but it's a useful writing exercise for any occasion. The discipline of conveying detail in a few words is a good tool to use in all aspects of your writing and, if you're struggling with a blank page, it can serve as both a distraction and a way to get some words down on paper, hopefully lifting the dreaded block.

Write on anything you like, but if love inspires you, in the 17 syllables of a haiku, tell us why your Valentine is so very special. Or why you're so right in being anti-Valentine.

In case you're in need of a prompt, a haiku is a Japanese poem with three short lines of five, seven, and five syllables.

Matsuo Basho is said to have been a master of them. Some of his (not always altogether intelligible) works are below.

> *the first cold shower*
>
> *even the monkey seems to want*
>
> *a little coat of straw*
>
> *the wind of Mt. Fuji*
>
> *I've brought on my fan!*
>
> *a gift from Edo*
>
> *old pond*
>
> *a frog jumps*
>
> *the sound of water*

No epics of courtly love, no novels in verse, and no sonnets, please. Vent or exalt, but do it in no more than 17 syllables.

# TEN

The Kanun is a set of traditional Albanian laws, begun in oral form and remaining unwritten until the 19th century. One of its edicts is that families remain patrilineal and patrilocal – wealth is inherited by the male members of the family and, upon marriage, the women move into the household of their husbands' families, becoming their property. These marriages may be arranged, at birth or in early childhood. Women may, however, become men by taking a vow under the law of the Kanun to become a virgjëresha – a "sworn virgin". They must remain celibate and unmarried, acting, dressing, talking, and working like a man, and assuming the responsibilities of head of the household when they are of age, including those incurred by a blood feud. The reasons for taking this vow are usually to avoid an arranged marriage or because the family require it due to a lack of sons. Women may also choose to take the vow because they feel more comfortable living as a man. They will not marry or have children, but by taking the vow they are considered men and provided with the rights, freedoms, and opportunities traditionally given only to men under the Kanun.

What would the life of a virgjëresha be like in your own culture? Would the life of a woman living as a man be markedly different to that of a woman who had not taken the vow? What about a male virgjëresha? Reverse the role and consider the life of a man who had taken a vow to live as a woman and be regarded by society as one.

# ELEVEN

In France it is forbidden to call a pig Napoleon; in England it is legal to murder a Scotsman within the ancient city walls of York, but only if he is carrying a bow and arrow; in San Salvador, drunk drivers can be executed by firing squad; in Indonesia, the penalty for masturbation is decapitation; in Vermont, women must obtain written permission from their husbands to wear false teeth; and in Florida, it is illegal to have sex with a porcupine. Peculiar laws offer both entertainment and a fascinating insight into historical customs. As an exercise in research (and as a way to put off writing that feels productive), see if you can find ten strange laws.

# TWELVE

Novels about novelists are an intriguing mix of autobiography (or material that is assumed to be autobiographical) and fiction. Writers drop in hints of their own lives – David Copperfield starting his writing career as a journalist reporting on parliamentary debates as did Charles Dickens, the religious conflicts in The End of the Affair could mirror Graham Greene's own concerns about his faith, and Nathan Zuckerman's novel in Zuckerman Unbound sounds remarkably like the author's own succès de scandale, Portnoy's Complaint. With other writers it is more difficult to tell how much of themselves they've inserted into the narrative. You would hope that Stephen King never encountered the fate of Misery's Paul Sheldon or that George Gissing's life experience brought him anywhere close to the poverty and suicide of his novelist characters. Carol Shields' Unless could be a sly dig at the critics who were condescending towards her earlier writing and fragments of the secrets of Margaret Atwood's The Blind Assassin might be her own, but only she would know.

How would you write the story of a novelist? Would you write yourself into the character or include none of the details of your own life? Perhaps you would start with yourself as the basis of the character and embellish it. Or your own story may be sufficiently colourful and engaging that it requires no embellishment and need only be lightly fictionalised if you want to remain anonymous and write fiction rather than autobiography.

# THIRTEEN

These men are in a police identity parade. What did they do?

# FOURTEEN

Create an impression of a character using only a description of the face. Don't tell the reader what to think about the person. Show the traits you wish to convey through a physical description alone.

Think about facial characteristics and distinguishing marks. If a character has a scar, how did he get it? If she wears makeup, which parts of her face does she wish to accentuate and why? These explanations can be brief – you don't need to write the entire story behind the scar, for example. It just needs to be a short explanation that gives an indication of what the character is like. Describe how the character moves her mouth when she talks. Think about moods – happiness, sorrow, disappointment, delight. How would they appear on the character's face? Don't name the book or feeling. Instead, let it be conveyed through facial characteristics and movement.

# FIFTEEN

Choose a character trait – for example, lazy, forgetful, meticulous. Now choose a room in the house in which this character lives and describe it so it reveals the character trait. Don't mention whichever trait you choose. Try to convey it through the description. Don't parody the trait or labour the point with excessive detail. Don't inform the reader what the character is like – just give enough detail to suggest it. Choose four more character traits (or as many as you can think of that could be conveyed through a description of setting) and do the same. You can use the same room if you like or vary it so, for example, you describe a slovenly person's kitchen, a meticulous person's bedroom, and a forgetful person's study.

# SIXTEEN

Select an obituary from a newspaper and rewrite it, imagining what the subject's life might have been like if he or she had made different choices. You can make the scenarios as preposterous or as plausible as you like. Just keep writing, imagining how a life can develop and change according to the choices a person makes. Perhaps the person would have developed into someone entirely different if the events in his or her life had been different. Think about the common decisions made by people. For example, regarding marriage, work, where they live, if they have children, and pastimes. Then think about the more uncommon events and scenarios in their lives – the things that they had to consider and that took place, making their lives individual.

# SEVENTEEN

Look at the lonely hearts page in a newspaper or magazine. What do people write about themselves? They usually only give brief descriptions of what they're like and what they're looking for. Imagine the descriptions in more detail and match characters. What would happen if they met? Write their first encounter. You don't need to match the people you think would be most compatible – in fact, the encounters could be more interesting if the people were entirely incompatible based on their descriptions of themselves.

# EIGHTEEN

Imagine a day dressed in a hijab. How do you think people would respond to you? What would you see? How would it feel?

If you wear a hijab, imagine a day without it, dressed, for example, in jeans and a t-shirt. How would that feel? Do you think people would respond to and look at you differently?

# NINETEEN

Every day there are peculiar news stories. A glance through a single newspaper will reveal a myriad of tales. One such tale was of a man who, upon being rushed to hospital with a collapsed lung, was found to have a pea plant growing in his lung. It had, apparently, gone down the wrong way when he swallowed it and had then sprouted inside his lung, growing to a height of half an inch. Imagine the pea had never been found and write a story in which a plant – it can be a pea or any plant you wish – grew inside somebody. Look at it from different perspectives. If you write for children, you may, for example, write about a dog who grew flowers out of his ears. You could write it from the perspective of the person. Write it from a clinical perspective or make it surreal. It's a preposterous tale, but it's true so see where you can take it.

# TWENTY

Cinderella is an oft-told tale of justice, comeuppance, enchantment, and love. For her beauty and sweet nature, she is rewarded with marriage to a fine prince. What became of her?

# TWENTY ONE

What would you inspire a composer to write?

# TWENTY TWO

Daniel Defoe, Ezra Pound, Richard Lovelace, the Marquis de Sade, Jean Genet, Miguel de Cervantes, Sir Thomas Malory, John Bunyan, Oscar Wilde, and John Cleland all wrote while imprisoned for offences ranging from rape and public dissension, to theft, debt, and gross indecency. You've been sentenced to ten years' imprisonment with only pen and paper. What do you write?

# TWENTY THREE

Who is she?

# TWENTY FOUR

Sex scenes are notoriously difficult to write. They can end up laden with metaphors (moon grottos, diamond hard rods, and jade stalks), written in a style so clinical and with such microscopic detail they sound like extracts from medical textbooks, or disintegrating into non-words as the scene reaches its climax. To name a few of the ways in which a sex scene can go wrong. Men and women tend to write about sex differently, though if you don't know the gender of the author it isn't always easy to tell. Think about how you would write a sex scene. Decide the effect you want to create. Do you want it to be graphic or do you prefer to suggest, leaving it up to the reader to imagine the details? It could be humorous, intended to be comedic rather than erotic or, perhaps, you prefer poetic style. Write the scene then switch genders. If you are a man, write the scene as you think a woman would and, if you are a woman, write the scene as you think a man would write it.

# TWENTY FIVE

Identity theft tends to be considered a 20th and 21st century phenomenon. However, from the fictional reinvention of Edmond Dantès into the Count of Monte Cristo and the 18th century real-life mimicry of Jean Henri Latude to Frank Abagnale and Albert Gonzalez, creating an identity or stealing someone else's in order to conceal one's own is a centuries-old practice. If you could steal anyone's identity, who would you be?

# TWENTY SIX

Statistical reports can be useful sources of information and spark for characters. They are studies of the ordinary that offer the possibility to create the extraordinary by writing the stories behind them. Studies show that even the most unhappy couples become closer on holiday; being lonely and alone is as bad for your health as smoking 15 cigarettes a day; the ideal duration for sex is 7-13 minutes with anything over three minutes described as "adequate" and over thirteen minutes as "too long"; divorce rates vary according to occupation with dentists among those least likely to get divorced at only 8%, to dancers, 43% of whom are divorced; there are 27 oil spills across the planet each day; people, on average, wait longer to get married than they did in the 1990s; a survey of male drivers showed that 11% of men have their non-driving hand on their crotch. Analyses of dating websites reveal intriguing statistics about how people market themselves and what is considered attractive. For example, an analysis of OK Cupid found that 80% of people who categorised themselves as bisexual were actually only interested in one gender. A study of the "hit rates" (the number of times a person's profile is viewed) for dating site shots show that women with cats get 24% fewer hits, but men with a dog get 50% more. Women showing cleavage get 43% more and men with muscles on show increase their hit rate by 45%. If a woman's occupation is considered "interesting", a man is 48% more likely to start an online conversation with her.

Statistics may look like nothing more than figures and percentages, but each number represents human lives. Who are the people behind these studies? Where are the oil spills and who are the people living with them? Who is the woman with the cat in her profile picture and why does she find the muscular man more appealing than the thin one? What happened on holiday that made the couple decide not to get divorced? Why do dancers get more divorced more frequently than dentists? Everything has a backstory.

## TWENTY SEVEN

Imagine a day in the life of someone else. Don't write it as if you are yourself – write it as you think they would experience their days. What would the life of a stay-at-home mother be like? What does a despot eat for breakfast? Does a poet dream in metaphors? What is the journey to work like for an accountant living in Baghdad? How slowly do the hours spent in meditation pass for a monk in a Tibetan monastery? What does a vicar think when he looks at his congregation? How does a circus ring-mistress feel as she steps into the ring? There are billions of lives from which you could choose. Spend a day living one.

## TWENTY EIGHT

At the age of thirteen, Jordan Romero became the youngest person to climb Mount Everest. It's an environment and activity that, prior to Romero's climb, had been experienced by adults alone. Put children into adult situations and write it from their perspective. Send them off to climb mountains, run a board meeting or go to the supermarket. How would these experiences appear from a child's point of view?

# TWENTY NINE

Life everlasting. Would you live forever if you could?

# THIRTY

Child beauty pageants are a multimillion-dollar industry. To some they are a harmless pastime; to others, they are a way in which to instil girls with self esteem and confidence; and to some they are exploitative and inappropriate, forcing children to act in a sexual manner and believe that physical appearance is the most important aspect of their lives. Whatever your particular opinion on the subject, forget it and imagine a day at a pageant. Choose a single contestant and follow her through the day. Write it from different points of view: the child, the parent, a judge, another contestant, the parent of another contestant. How does each person perceive the event?

# THIRTY ONE

Envy is a troublesome emotion. Though expressing one's envy is generally acceptable, depending on what it is you are envious of, acting on it may not be. When was the first time you felt envious? What or who were you envious of, how did it make you feel, and what did you do about it?

# THIRTY TWO

Love everlasting. You might crave it, be living it, believe it to be a Hallmark invention, ponder it, or know it to be a lie. To find out what keeps people together, interview couples who have been with each other a long time. Make 40 years the minimum duration of their relationship. See what they can tell you about how long love can last. If you've been together that long, maybe you already know the secret.

# THIRTY THREE

What do you see when you look in the mirror?

# THIRTY FOUR

Choose two historical figures and send them on a blind date. Write the date from three perspectives: someone watching it and each of the two figures. The person watching can be you as an omniscient author or a person in the same venue, looking on. Write it in the first person from the perspective of each figure. What were their impressions of each other? What did they talk about? How did the date progress? Did they go on anywhere after it? Would they meet again? From marks out of ten, how did they rate each other?

# THIRTY FIVE

"For sale: baby shoes, never worn." This six-word story by Ernest Hemingway is a flash fiction classic. In only eight syllables, there is a myriad of tales and images. Start with 100 words. Write a story of that length, then keep cutting until you get to 20 (or six, if you can manage it). Is your story still intact? Does it still contain the key elements - character, plot, and setting - with which you started? As you cut words, you will have to imply more than you write. In addition to being a way in which to put off whatever it is you're supposed to be doing, it is also a good exercise in discipline because it makes you hone down your writing, conveying a tale to the reader without crowding your work with unnecessary detail.

# THIRTY SIX

Spend a day blind. Don't cheat by opening your eyes and don't stay in your home. Go out. Walk the streets with which you familiar. Do the tasks you normally do, but keep your eyes closed or covered. Take a friend with you as a guide – to stop you walking in front of buses, for example – or go out alone. How would you cope without sight? Imagine varying scenarios: if you had been blind from birth, lost your sight suddenly, or felt it fade gradually. How would you describe your world if you couldn't see it? How would you experience it?

# THIRTY SEVEN

Genetic Sexual Attraction (GSA) is the name given to two members of the same biological family meeting as adults and having a sexual relationship. Cultural responses to it vary: in some it is regarded as an acceptable practice and legal right, in others it is taboo, and in some it is illegal. Write the story of siblings, raised apart, who meet as adults and have a sexual relationship, perhaps falling in love. Think of the possible scenarios. Make them heterosexual or homosexual. They might be strangers who meet and only discover later that they are siblings or they might have known of one another since childhood then met, knowing their biological relationship. How do they respond to each other and to their feelings? How does their family respond to their relationship? Is it legal or could they be imprisoned for an affair? Do they have children? Do they keep it secret or can they live openly as a couple? What are the consequences of the relationship?

# THIRTY EIGHT

Your character's great love is a life-sized doll. What is their life like? What sort of doll is it – cloth, robotic, silicone? Can it talk? Why does your character love it?

# THIRTY NINE

Write the story of the relationship between a famous figure and a lesser known person with whom they were involved. Explore a real relationship – between artist Elizabeth Shoumatoff and Franklin D. Roosevelt, Colette and her companion, Pauline, or between Gertrude Stein and her brother, Leo, for example. Or you could fictionalise a character who would have existed but about whom little or nothing is known. The bartender at La Bodeguita del Medio in Havana where Ernest Hemingway drank, Benito Mussolini's chef, or Coco Chanel's chambermaid at the Ritz in Paris. Alternatively, you could write about a contemporary figure: Katie Price's nanny, Muammar Abu Minyar al-Gaddafi's bodyguard, or Ridley Scott's on-set assistant. You don't have to use these examples. Think about people who intrigue you and imagine the relationship. What do they talk about? What do the assistants, secretaries, nannies, bodyguards, bartenders, siblings, and cleaners see? Are they close? Do they like each other? Did they laugh at each other? What is their relationship like?

# FORTY

Your characters can never go home. Why not?

# FORTY ONE

Comedy has a reputation for being difficult to write, but that doesn't mean you shouldn't try. What is the funniest thing that's ever happened to you or that you've done? See how many people you can make laugh in the re-telling. Remember, you have to make other people laugh. Don't just say, "You really had to be there". Even if you find it so hilarious, you laugh until you feel sick, you have to make it funny for other people, too.

# FORTY TWO

People meet in peculiar places and in peculiar ways. They cycle into each other and land in a heap on the pavement; a woman helps a man out of a hot air balloon after it crashes in her garden; they meet in war zones, hospitals, circuses, and supermarkets. Write the story of your strangest meeting. If you have never had one, then write the story of characters who have. Make it an outlandish scenario or a seemingly everyday one that began an unlikely pairing.

# FORTY THREE

Death bed regrets. Among those most common are wishing one had maintained friendships, spent less time at work and more with family and partners, expressed one's feelings, allowed oneself to feel happier, and lived a life of one's own choosing rather than that expected by others. What will your characters die wishing they had or hadn't done?

# FORTY FOUR

Family is an intriguing subject both for writers and readers because it is, at once, familiar and unfamiliar, ordinary and extraordinary. In fiction, there are wicked uncles, beastly stepmothers, kindly fathers, unhinged mothers, irresistible sisters, shell-shocked brothers, banished grandmothers, and murderous aunts. In reality, there are all these figures and many more. Your own family can be a source of inspiration with its relationships, dynamics, and individuals. To you, they will simply be a part of your everyday life, but every family is different. To the outsider, they may not be ordinary at all. Look at different members of your family. Write portraits of them. Write snapshots of them as they are now or at moments in their lives. Look at their pasts and write lengthier tales or write snapshots of them as they were at different points in their past. If you're writing frank accounts, people might not be happy with how you depict them so do be prepared for some negative responses. If you intend to publish material based upon those close to you, unless you really don't care about the consequences of purloining parts of friends and relatives, exercise a little caution. For the sake of authenticity, it isn't necessary to turn writing into a blood sport.

# FORTY FIVE

Imagine a life lived in front of an audience. Make it a camera or a live audience, as though the life were being lived on a stage. The audience follows the individual for every moment of the day. What does it see and how does the person feel?

# FORTY SIX

Write a life as a video game. Make yourself a character in it, if you like, perhaps embellishing yourself with abilities and characteristics. Create scenarios within the game. The way a life could be and what it could have in it are infinite. Reflect your real life or transform it in a world in which nothing is real and there are none of the restrictions of realism or reality.

# FORTY SEVEN

Take any article from a newspaper – review, news, interview, obituary, feature, opinion piece, letter to the editor, problem page, or column. Cut up all the words and rearrange them to form a story. Can you create a narrative with random words?

# FORTY EIGHT

Poltergeists are usually supporting parts in writing, but what if your narrator was one? What is your poltergeist? What form does it take? Can it talk, hear, see? Can people see it? How do they react and what does your poltergeist think of their reactions? Does it interact with them? Many theories exist as to the origins of poltergeists: they are an external manifestation of psychological trauma, they are passed on from person to person, or they embed themselves in a place where a person died in a rage or with conflicts unresolved. Perhaps your poltergeist has a story of its own. Intersperse the tales it tells with its actions and the people around it.

# FORTY NINE

Poetry and sport aren't subjects that are usually associated with one another. That doesn't mean you can't use sport as a subject for a poem, though. No matter what your opinion of sport, it's something about which you could write. Whatever you feel – passion, ambivalence, indifference, loathing – make it the subject of a poem. Write about a sporting moment you'll never forget, the boy you're in love with on the school football team, the boringness of the World Cup as it drags on for weeks, your own sporting achievement or lack there-of, your row of cups kept polished in a cabinet, the irritating kids who keep kicking a football into your garden, rained-off baseball games, soccer moms, big-bellied men shouting at the television. Imagine yourself in the mind of an athlete as she prepares for a race or, if you'd like to write from the perspective of an animal, that of the horse as it waits at the post. You could write about your opinions of a particular sport. Hunting, for example – is it cruel, necessary, or simply entertaining? Write a love sonnet to cricket, a haiku about how much you hate your swimming instructor, or free verse on football fans.

# FIFTY

An artist has been commissioned to paint a portrait of you or a picture inspired by you. If an artist looked at you and your life, what would you inspire him or her to create?

# FIFTY ONE

2010 marked the 50th anniversary of the publication of To Kill A Mockingbird. For some people it was a book of tremendous social and political significance, for others it was a great read, and for many it was the dullest book in the universe but one they had to read for school. However you regard the book, it is still an oft-cited text and has remained a classic. As an exercise in using autobiographical material in your writing, think of a book that had significance in your life. It might just have meant something to you at the time or it might have changed your life irrevocably. Recapture, if you can, the feelings the book created and why it had an effect upon you. Remember - don't just write a list of feelings and thoughts. The idea is to enable the reader to experience the book as you did.

# FIFTY TWO

Talismans are objects believed to offer protection and good luck to their owners. There are official talismans like the kimi-yah, bulla, gemstone, crucifix, four-leafed clover, omamori, ta'wiz, jackal's horn, and rabbit's foot. And there are others created by people with their own meanings – from papier-mâché dolls and lucky shoes to poems worn in lockets and painted stones. What would your talisman be and what powers would you give to it?

The Fine Line is an Edinburgh-based editorial consultancy and publisher, committed to helping new, burgeoning, and established writers realise their literary potential. Our aim is to inspire and assist. We provide advice to get you started, lessons to download, insights into the methods of working writers, writing prompts, a Dear Editor writers' problem page, mentoring, and an editorial service designed for your individual needs.

If you would like feedback on writing generated by the prompts, or any other work, it can be submitted through the Fine Line site at http://editorial-consultancy.co.uk/.

# NOTES

# NOTES

# NOTES

# NOTES

# NOTES

# NOTES

# NOTES

# NOTES

# NOTES

# NOTES

# NOTES

# NOTES

# NOTES

www.ingramcontent.com/pod-product-compliance
Lightning Source LLC
Chambersburg PA
CBHW020953030426
42339CB00004B/72